Roberta's QuickSta

For Smaller Decision-Making Groups in Business and Nonprofits

Work Groups, Boards of Directors, Advisory Councils, Citizen Panels or Commissions, Committees, Teams and Task Forces

A companion workbook to

Roberta's Rules of Order™

by

Alice Collier Cochran, M.Ed.

Published by Jossey-Bass, a Wiley Imprint, 2004

To Implement Parts II and III

Effective Decision Making

and

Easy Meeting Methods

Dedication

This Guide is dedicated to the late Caroline Sizer (Cally) Cochran, the best mother-in-law and civic role model a woman could have!

In the 1950's she pioneered "Population Education" to teach family planning in the public schools of Baltimore, Maryland. If only her impact had been worldwide!

Cally served on many boards in the Washington-Baltimore area. Her brother-in-law Sturgis Warner wrote a story spoofing Cally's involvement in nonprofits called *Cally's Diary.* An excerpt reads:

> *Left at 9:03 AM to act as chair of League of Women Voters meeting.*
> *Gave my speech on "Some Observations on Parliamentary*
> *Procedure in Maryland's Women's Organizations" and drafted the*
> *platform for the League for next six years.*

Cally Cochran always thought that meetings should be both productive and FUN! I believe she would have welcomed the use of Roberta's Rules in the meetings she attended.

Alice Collier Cochran

San Rafael, California

Roberta's QuickStart Guide

CONTENTS

Introduction

Why Use This Guide?

Having seen firsthand the frustration of many members of nonprofit boards, committees, and business teams, I wrote *Roberta's Rules of Order* (Jossey-Bass, 2004) as an alternative to using parliamentary procedure in civic and business meetings of small groups.

Parliamentary-based methods are most appropriate in large groups, not small ones. Unfortunately, it's been misapplied in many nonprofit boards, committees, special councils, and teams, leaving people feeling too controlled and often confused.

I've developed this step-by-step Guide for readers who have said, "We love Roberta's Rules, we're a small group, and we want to shift to a more informal and interactive method, but *how do we do it?*" My intention is to make it easier for any group desiring to make this change. This Guide is for *you*.

Use a Compass to Get Your Bearings

Ships use a compass to stay on course. The companion book *Roberta's Rules of Order* was organized around the four major directions of a compass, as illustrated on page 19. This Guide, designed around a **new** compass (see next page) with eight points, will help you to implement two sections of Roberta's Rules:

Part II: Navigate Decision Making Through Rough Waters (Chapters 3–5)

pages 33 through 76.

Part III: Select Easy Meeting Methods to Get All Hands on Deck (Chapters 6–9)

pages 79 through 139.

A New Compass for This Guide

This QuickStart Guide is divided into **eight** compass points (called **Steps** throughout) that will help you implement Part II and Part III of *Roberta's Rules of Order*.

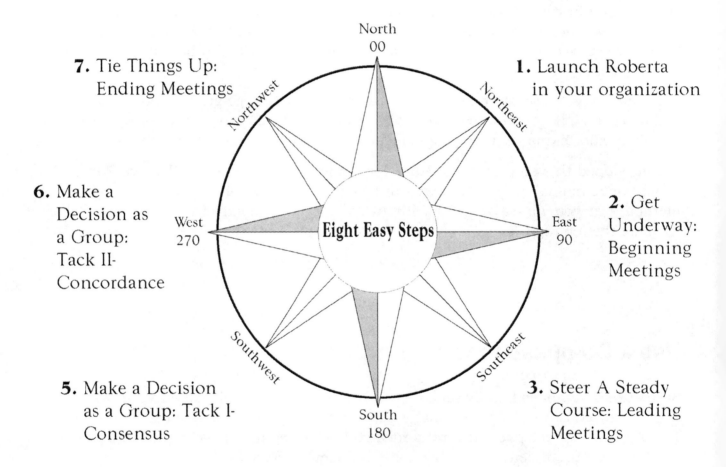

8. Customize Roberta:
Your Meeting Method

7. Tie Things Up:
Ending Meetings

1. Launch Roberta
in your organization

6. Make a
Decision as
a Group:
Tack II-
Concordance

2. Get
Underway:
Beginning
Meetings

5. Make a Decision
as a Group: Tack I-
Consensus

3. Steer A Steady
Course: Leading
Meetings

4. Prepare a Proposal
for Action

North
00

Northwest

Northeast

West
270

Eight Easy Steps

East
90

Southwest

Southeast

South
180

Sailing Ships and the Sea Analogy

Because of my interest in the sea and sailing traditionally rigged ships, I enjoy using related analogies. The English language is full of terms that were derived from the sea and sailing.

Have you ever heard someone say "We've gone overboard on this"? Or when money is tight, "We need to batten down the hatches"? In this Guide you'll find nautical references. If this seems strange, please use a different analogy... like golf.

This artwork by Scott Kennedy, "Twin Brigantines at Angel's Gate," shows the youth sail-training tall ships, *Irving Johnson and Exy Johnson,* owned and operated by the Los Angeles Maritime Institute (LAMI). Used with permission.

Optimize or Change Your Meeting Culture

My purpose is to help you support—or perhaps change—your organization's meeting "culture." A group's culture is made up of a series of habits. They may be helping or hindering you in getting work done.

Think of a culture as being like a community on an island. If you want to move from one type of meeting culture to another, you can do so by "shifting shores" from the culture described in the list on the left (Move Away From...) to the culture described in the list on the right (Move Toward...). This Guide will help you make that shift.

If your group's culture already fits the list on the right, this Guide will help you codify a complementary method for planning and "steering" your meetings.

Move Away From . . .	*Move Toward . . .*
Formality	Informality
Strict rules	Guidelines and agreements
Parliamentary procedures	Democratic principles and processes
Language of 1900s	Common usage of 2000s
Military influence	Civilian influence
One size fits all	Flexible
Win-lose voting	Win-win decisions
Two decision choices (yes or no)	Straw polls and multiple choices
Controlled	Relaxed
Complicated	Simple
Debate	Dialogue and conversation
Motions as solutions	Proposals *precede* a motion

Overall Objectives

Complete all the points of the compass, and your group will:

- Decide *Roberta's Rules* is appropriate for your group

- Plan an agenda, using a simple format with the focus on your mission

- Steer discussions to get results

- Develop a proposal to inform everyone of a problem or opportunity, before making a motion

- Decide among several decision-making options, depending on the situation

- Tie things down at the end of a meeting to implement actions

- Customize a set of rules or guidelines for your meetings

Develop Your Own Rules

Although there are many versions of parliamentary procedure adapted for use in nonprofit or NGO (nongovernmental organization) meetings, *Robert's Rules of Order,* by Gen. Henry M. Robert (a U.S. Army engineer) is the best known. It's also a good "branding" story.

The original title, more than 130 years ago, was "The Pocket Manual of Rules of Order for Deliberative Assemblies." After self-publication under this name, a publisher with a marketing eye changed the title to a more memorable one: *Robert's Rules of Order.* That's the good news. The bad news is that over the years the "pocket manual" has grown from his original intent of 16 pages to over 600 pages!

It's important to know that parliamentary-based procedures were derived from an ancient Anglo-Saxon method intended for deliberative assemblies. These are large voting bodies, such as state legislatures and the senate or house of the U.S. Congress (whose rules, by the way, differ). Another example is a convention of delegates from all the chapters of a national or international association.

The Introduction to the tenth edition of Robert's Rules of Order (2000) states that these rules are not intended for groups as small as about a dozen members. Organizations that do not wish to have the formality of parliamentary procedure are encouraged to write their own "special rules"—but who has time?

Save Yourself Time

You don't have to write your own rules! Use Roberta's Rules and customize them. I've included many of the templates from the Resources section in the back of *Roberta's Rules of Order* and added some new ones, to make them easy to customize. For your convenience, I've included relevant sections from the book and referenced other material by chapter and page numbers.

Every member of a group should have his or her own QuickStart Guide to complete, and the group should have at least one copy of *Roberta's Rules of Order* as a resource. In this group activity, I encourage you to share the role of reading the information aloud to each other. This activity increases listening, comprehension, and memory.

Select Your Schedule

This Guide for implementing Roberta's Rules is formatted for smaller decision-making groups to be "done in a day." There are eight steps, each approximately one hour long. If you follow this self-paced Guide from start to finish, you can fully implement Roberta's Rules in one daylong meeting, or in a series of shorter meetings over weeks or months.

Choose the timing that works for your group. The steps are in logical order, but you could complete them in any order. Feel free to skip any step that seems redundant, based on your current practices.

Your options are:

• A one day meeting (Done-in-a-Day) format

• One hour a month, over eight month

• Two hours a month, over four months

• Or another choice that works for your group

In Step One, you'll be asked to choose the schedule that works best for your group. Above all, make it practical, and have fun.

If you are only looking for a meeting and decision-making method to agree upon and use in your business meetings, go directly to Step Eight and customize these rules. (Check out the example customized by a nonprofit in the Resources.) You'll be done in an hour!

Each Step Follows This Pattern

To make this implementation Guide easy to follow, each step follows the same sequence of sections:

- **Introduction:** What happens in this step?

- **Purpose of This Step**: Why do it?

- **Checklist of Results**: What you will accomplish in this step

- **Resource:** A chapter or section to read in *Roberta's Rules of Order*

- **Information** you'll need to read to use in the step (and read it aloud together)

- **An Agenda** for each session that includes what do to (using a worksheet) and suggested timeframes

- **A Worksheet**, with instructions that correspond to the agenda

By completing the Worksheet at the end of each section, you'll have the conversations and make the decisions that will help you move to the next step. The culminating step is Step Eight, where you will use these decisions to customize and adopt your own meeting guidelines.

YOU'VE COMPLETED THE INTRODUCTION. NOW YOU'RE READY TO GO TO STEP ONE, **LAUNCH ROBERTA'S RULES: GETTING STARTED.**

NOTES:

Launch Roberta's Rules: Getting Started

Step One

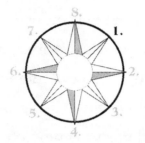

Introduction

This is your first step in applying Roberta's Rules in your organization, and customizing rules for your own use (which is Step Eight).

Before going further, it's important to decide if your organization wants to shift to, or support, the meeting culture as seen on the right in the side-by-side comparison in the Introduction on page 10. Roberta's Rules are based on a set of beliefs and values that will feel comfortable only if they are compatible with your organization's beliefs and values.

Also in this session, you'll start developing some good meeting habits, such as sharing roles, using courtesy guidelines, and pledging to one another to use communication skills toward developing trust and maintaining relationships.

Purpose of This Step

Use Step One to decide whether to begin using Roberta's Rules in your organization—and if so, know how to get started.

Checklist of Results

By completing Step One, you will:

☐ Decide who will be your first Leader, to guide you through this agenda, and your Timekeeper, to help you stay on time

☐ Review the beliefs and key principles on which Roberta's Rules is based

☐ Decide if Roberta is compatible with your organization

☐ If you proceed, decide which Courtesy Guidelines you'll use in future meetings

☐ Adopt a Communication Pledge with your group's members

☐ Decide how and when you'll meet to complete this Guide to Roberta's Rules

Resource in *Roberta*

From *Roberta's Rules of Order*, please read the Introduction and pages 27 and 28.

Information You'll Need to Use

Beliefs That Support Roberta's Rules

Roberta's Rules are based on a number of beliefs:

- People tend to support what they help create, or at least influence

- Starting with the problem is more logical than starting with the solution (a motion is a solution)

- Solutions that allow most who are involved to "win" are worth striving for

- Consensus isn't always worth the struggle (but it is a good beginning)

- Productive interaction can arise out of mild chaos

- Everyone has something to offer and should express it—once

- The wisdom of the group is discovered through logically structured (not random) conversation

Key Principles

There are seven fundamental principles that serve as a foundation for Roberta's Rules.

1. Use simple meeting methods
2. Structure minimally
3. Share roles and responsibilities
4. Strive for substantial agreement
5. Shift from debate to dialogue
6. Show respect for different ways of thinking
7. Stay focused on the current mission and the future

Share Responsibility: Rotate Roles in Meetings

For Step One, there are two roles: the **Leader** and the **Timekeeper.**

The **Leader** keeps the group focused on the agenda and follows the process. The leader can be the formal leader, such as board president or team leader, or any other willing person.

The **Timekeeper's** job is to keep the group conscious of time. He or she reminds the group when it is 1 or 2 minutes before the end of a discussion.

Use Courtesy Guidelines

Often called "Groundrules," the following are intended to help a group respect one another in a meeting. These are samples, so you can confirm or change these to what feels appropriate for your group. The following are some examples; use these or develop your own.

- Share the "airtime" by keeping our remarks to three minutes and then letting others talk (use a silent hourglass-type egg timer)

- Avoid interrupting others; give each person three minutes

- Limit the dialogue between two people to two exchanges, and then open it up to include others

- Focus as a group on one part of the agenda at a time; create a list for other topics to be discussed outside the meeting or put on the agenda at the next meeting

- Avoid side conversations that distract others from listening to the person speaking

- Turn off cell phones and computers to help stay focused and have eye contact

Have a Communication Agreement

Every group has the intention of communicating well, but also the potential not to do so. We've all seen it happen! When communication breaks down, people pull back, disengage, and often stop coming to meetings.

The following Communication Agreement is a sample statement of expectations of how board members should treat each other during and outside of meetings. If things go badly, this pledge can be a reminder of the group's intended positive communication.

Communication Agreement

As long as I am a member of _____ I agree to:

1) Speak to and about others, as I want them to speak to or about me.

2) Assume the best (rather than the worst) about others' intentions until I know otherwise.

3) Listen as an ally (rather than an adversary) to understand the point of view of others whether or not I agree with it.

4) Speak my own opinion in a way that does not demean others, even if I disagree.

5) Speak for myself, using "I" messages and not blaming statements.

6) Refrain from using aggressive verbal or nonverbal behavior or sarcasm when I do not agree with someone.

7) Keep confidential what is said in our meetings about others, particularly when it could be hurtful to any individual.

8) Follow the Courtesy Guidelines in Meetings, adopted by this group.

9)

10)

Signature: _____ Date: _____

Agenda for Step One

Sections	Method or Directions	Estimated Time
Transition	Refreshments and conversation	15–30 min.
Start the meeting	Answer question #1 in the Step One Worksheet	5–10 min.
Purpose Intended results	Leader: Review purpose and meeting checklist	5–10 min.
Agenda	Review the full agenda; adjust times as needed	
Rationale for Roberta's Rules	Read the Introduction aloud	10–15 min.
Beliefs and principles of Roberta's Rules	Complete #2 in Worksheet	10–15 min.
Using the compass to chart a course	Review the eight steps in the Guide; decide on your self-paced schedule Complete #3	5–15 min.
Courtesy Guidelines	Complete #4	10–15 min.
Communication Pledge	Complete #5	5–10 min.
Reflect	Complete #6	5–10 min.
Conclude	Complete #7	5–10 min.

Step One Worksheet

Please complete these questions and directions, using the **Agenda for Step One**.

1. Sharing the Roles

- Who will be the Leader to guide the group in this step?

  _____

- Who will be the Timekeeper?

  _____

- How often will we rotate these roles?

  _____

2. Beliefs and Key Principles

- Do they fit our group? _____

- How do they fit with our current culture?

  _____

- Are they compatible enough to proceed?

  _____

3. Meeting Schedule to Adopt Roberta? (Review Options in the Introduction)

- What meeting schedule shall we use?

  _____

- How often will we meet? _____

4. Courtesy Guidelines

- Which shall we use? All of them? some? add others?

- Suggested Courtesy Guidelines for meetings—we will:

  Share the "airtime" by keeping our remarks to three minutes and then letting others talk (use a silent hourglass-type egg timer)

  Avoid interrupting others; give each person three minutes

  Limit the dialogue between two people to two exchanges, and then open it up to include others

  Focus as a group on one part of the agenda at a time; create a list for other topics to be discussed outside the meeting or put on the agenda at the next meeting

  Avoid side conversations that distract others from listening to the person speaking

  Turn off cell phones and computers to help stay focused and have eye contact

  Others:

  _____

_____

_____

5. **Communication Pledge**

   • Please read the Communication Pledge in this section and modify it so you and all other group members are comfortable. Once it's agreed on, sign the pledge.

6. **Reflect**

   • How did we do? _____

   • What methods worked well at this first meeting and should be used repeatedly?
     _____

   • What didn't work as well and should be changed?
     _____

   • What changes shall we make, and how? (Reach agreement.)
     _____

7. **Conclude**

   • Wrap up. Are there any actions to complete as follow-up on this meeting? If yes, complete the chart; expand it if necessary.

What to Do	By Whom	By When

   • Return to the Checklist of Results at the beginning of this step and check all items.

   • Who will take the same roles at the next meeting?

     Leader _____ Timekeeper _____

   • What do we need to read or do in advance?

     From *Roberta's Rules of Order,* please read Chapter Seven, "Respecting Everyone's Time by Steering a Steady Course," pages 95–114.

YOU'VE COMPLETED STEP ONE. NOW GO TO STEP TWO, **GET UNDER WAY: BEGINNING MEETINGS.**

Get Under Way: Beginning Meetings

Step Two

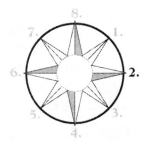

Introduction

Even though each part of a meeting is important, the beginning is crucial to accomplishing results at the end. What's often neglected is conscious attention to the process, as well as the content. Process is "how" a meeting is conducted—the flow, the tone, the seating, and the climate. Content is "what," or information including the intended results, topics, and topics to be discussed.

Think of a coin with "process" on one side and "content" on the other. They are different but inseparable. Process is often ignored in the beginning of a meeting, but it has a large impact on the success of the whole meeting. When I've asked any group about the "problems with their meetings" and made a list, they agree that the list includes over 80% process problems, not problems with content.

Step Two includes setting up the meeting in the most successful way before you convene and two "spokes" of a diagram called Ship's Wheel for Steering Meetings:

Convene the Meeting and **Help People Connect.**

The other "spokes" will be discussed in later steps.

Purpose of This Step

This step helps you start your meetings in a friendly, positive, and uplifting way, so that you will get the most cooperation and achieve the best results.

Checklist of Results

By completing Step Two, you will:

☐ Be familiar with using a ship's wheel as an analogy for managing meetings

☐ Decide how to share responsibility for the success of your meetings

☐ Know how to arrange seating for optimal eye contact

☐ Decide who should attend and each person's role

Resource in *Roberta*

From *Roberta's Rules of Order,* read Chapter Seven, "Respecting Everyone's Time by Steering a Steady Course," especially on the Ship's Wheel graphic, pages 102–104; and "Streamlining Discussions with a Clear Destination," Chapter Twelve.

Information You'll Need to Use

The diagram of the Ship's Wheel for Steering Meetings (on the next page) and the explanation that follows about each space between the spokes will give you the information you'll need for this section.

Ship's Wheel for Steering Meetings

This graphic gives a series of steps to use during meetings. The sequence in the following steps begins with **Convene the Meeting** in this step and concludes with **Complete an Expanded Agenda** in Step Eight. Please see the next page for definitions.

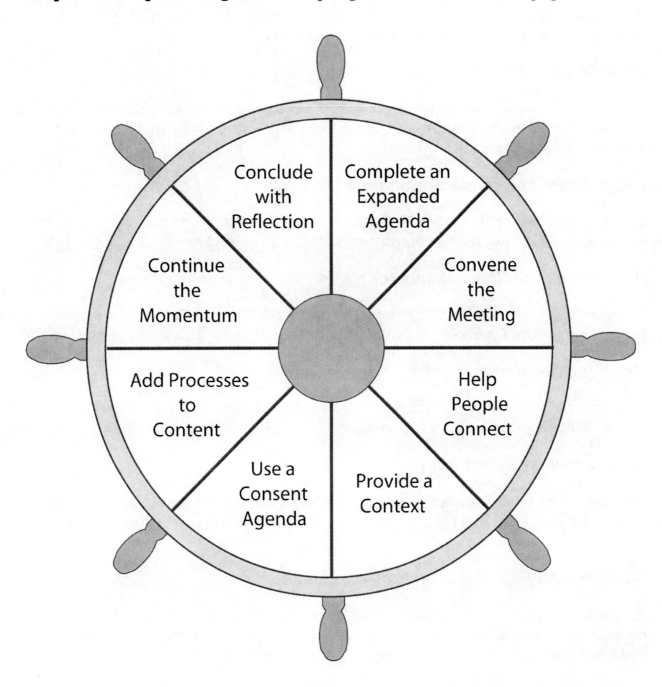

Convene the Meeting ☑

How you start the meeting is important. This section covers the "preventative" things to do before everyone starts to discuss the topics on the agenda.

Help People Connect ☑

Designating time for relaxing so as to transition into the meeting, as well as a structured check-in for everyone to speak, is helpful.

Provide a Context ☑

Knowing what's going on outside the group or has happened since the last meeting everyone focus on the present and the future. This includes furnishing information in advance via the Internet.

Use a Consent Agenda or Calendar ☑

This is a method for "bundling" items that need approval (consent) but do not require discussion. An example is a committee report sent in advance.

Add Process to Content and Topics ☑

Discussing a topic can lead anywhere (or nowhere) unless you have a method for using topics as a group. Examples are analyzing pros and cons, and prioritizing using "dots".

Continue the Momentum ☑

Momentum gained in a meeting can be lost unless there is a clear action plan and follow through. Always put a review of the Action Plan on the next meeting's agenda.

Conclude with Reflection ☑

Meetings often end in a rush. It's helpful to pause to say what was accomplished, who deserves acknowledgment, what went well, and what needs to be improved for the next meeting.

Complete an Expanded Agenda ☑

At the end of each meeting, begin to develop the agenda for the next. "Expanded" means that there is more information (like questions and timing) to help stay on track - not more work!

Decisions to Make Before a Meeting

Room Arrangement Options

How a meeting room is arranged is one of the biggest factors in group interaction, yet this simple adjustment of space is often overlooked. People strain unnecessarily to see and hear each other. The purpose of any room arrangement is to allow the maximum amount of eye contact and a clear line of sight to any information.

A few rules of thumbs are:

- The leader should be seated in the center of the group, not at the end of a table.

- Tables don't have to touch each other on the corners. Arrange a semicircle or horseshoe shape, even with rectangular tables.

- If there is one large table, make the seating three-quarters of the way around, forming a semicircle. Use the long side as the front so no one is seated far away.

- Minimize distractions and keep focused, face the group away from any doors.

- Use the "long wall" of the room to post flipcharts or project information.

- For meetings where discussion is important, minimize the use of projected images on a screen (use handouts) and keep the group members facing each other.

Please consult the following room arrangement options (A-C) on the next two pages for ideas on how to set up your meeting room to improve the interaction and increase the positive tone of your meetings.

For example, a condominium association's board had always put the board members behind three connected rectangular tables with members of the association seated some distance apart in straight rows. By simply using Option C, the meeting tone changed from generally negative to more positive.

OPTION A

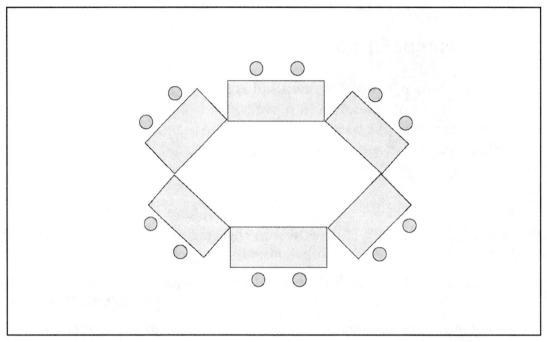

Seating with several tables for maximum eye contact

OPTION B

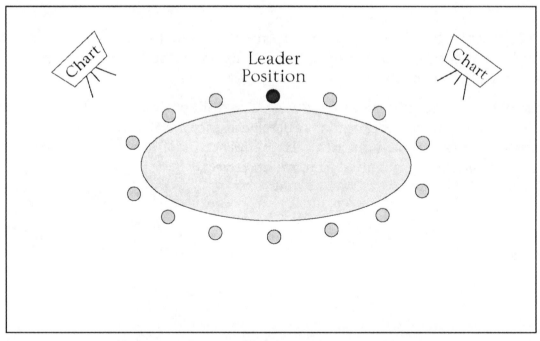

Seating with one table, oval or rectangular.
Leader is in center, not on end

OPTION C

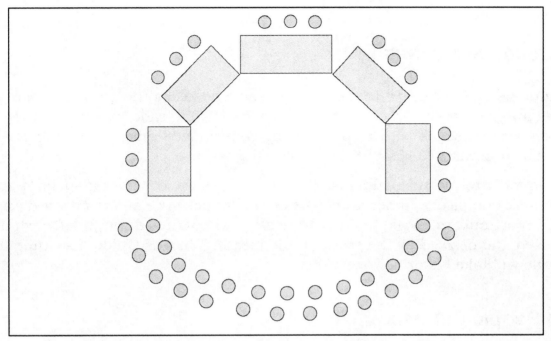

Open Meeting with Visitors

Who Should Attend?

If a board of directors of a membership organization is meeting. such as a condominium or neighborhood association, then members are free to attend. The same is true for public meetings that fall under the "sunshine law" within your state of incorporation. (Some states call it by a specific name, such as the Brown Act in California.) You can check with your secretary of state for guidelines.

Whenever there are invited guests or other visitors, it's important to welcome and introduce them to the group, and vice-versa. If at all possible, arrange for guest seating in an observer space around the perimeter of the room, rather than among the group members. This helps to clarify who is and who isn't part of the decision making.

Be clear in advance whether you want guests to participate in discussion or be silent observers. If participating, they are subject to the same Courtesy Guidelines that govern the group.

Convene the Meeting ☑

Continue using the roles of Leader (the person who keeps the group focused on the agenda and follows the process; this can be the formal leader or any other person) and Timekeeper (whose job is to keep the group conscious of time, reminding people when it's one or two minutes before the end of a discussion).

Add two more roles: the Egalitarian (who reinforces the courtesy guidelines and communication pledge, if necessary; he or she makes sure all are engaged and have an equal opportunity to speak) and the Notetaker, who writes down (briefly) what is discussed and decided by the group in the meeting. In this Guide, I assume that everyone will take his or her own notes.

Help People Connect ☑

When a meeting first begins people are often stressed from running late or thinking about other things. Tense participants often result in tense meetings.

Providing a transition time with food before the meeting is a great time for people to settle in and relax. Allow at least 30 minutes, with 15 for "slack time" to arrive and 15 to eat and socialize. Then start the meeting.

One thing to do at the beginning of the meeting to help people connect and relax is to have a brief "check in." The Leader poses a question with a time limit (30 seconds to one minute per person). Beware of conversations that may start; keep the process going.

The question should help reveal some personal (but not uncomfortable) information about others in the group, to build familiarity and trust.

A few example question are: What's been a highlight in your life since we've met? What are your vacation plans? How did you spend the holidays? etc.

If you want it to be focused on the organization, use questions like: What role do you naturally play in groups (observer, analyzer, etc.)? What values of this organization match your personal values?

Be creative and get to know each other on a deeper level to develop trust.

There are other things to when first convening the meeting, such as restating Courtesy Guidelines and making sure everyone understands the meetings purpose and intended results. These will be covered in Steps 3–8.

Agenda for Step Two

Sections	Method or Directions	Estimated Time
Transition Start the meeting	Refreshments and conversation	15–30 min.
Roles	Answer question #1 in Step Two Worksheet	5–10 min.
Purpose Intended results checklist Agenda Courtesy Guidelines	Leader: review purpose and checklist Review the full agenda; adjust times as needed Review and agree, or modify	5–10 min.
Content and process	Complete #2	10–15 min.
The Meeting Wheel	Review each section Read descriptions	10–15 min.
Before the meeting	Complete #3	20–30 min.
Reflect	Complete #4	5–10 min.
Conclude	Complete #5	5–10 min.

Step Two Worksheet

Please complete these questions and directions.

1. Sharing the Roles

- Who will be the next Leader?

  _____

- Who will be the Timekeeper? _____

- Who will be the Egalitarian? _____

2. Process and Content

- Is the explanation clear (yes or no)? _____

- Why is process important? _____

- Why is content important? _____

- What happens in a meeting when either is ignored?

  _____

3. Before the Meeting

Decide who to invite. Will we have regular participants, other than board members? Will we have guests to inform us about our field or other related work? List names of possible guests:

_____

_____

Plan the room arrangement. How can we arrange the room we use for maximum eye contact? (See options A-C.) How will we handle the seating of observers, guests, and other participants?

_____

_____

4. Reflect

Sharing responsibility. How are we doing sharing responsibility and rotating roles in these meetings? What can we improve?

_____

Using Courtesy guidelines. How are we doing using Courtesy Guidelines to speak and listen to each other? What can we improve?

_____

What methods worked well at this meeting that we should repeat?

_____

What didn't work as well that we could change?

_____

What changes shall we make, and how? (Reach agreement.)

_____

5. Conclude

- Wrap up. Are there any actions to complete in following up on this meeting?

What to Do	By Whom	By When

Return to the Checklist of Results at the beginning of this section and check all items.

- Who will take these roles at the next meeting?

Leader _____ Timekeeper _____

Egalitarian _____ Notetaker_____

- What do we need to read or do in advance?

From *Roberta's Rules of Order*, read "Respecting Everyone's Time by Steering a Steady Course" (Chapter Seven), the "Ship's Wheel" graphic, pp. 102–104; and "Streamlining Discussions with a Clear Destination," Chapter Twelve.

YOU'VE COMPLETED STEP TWO. NOW GO TO STEP THREE, **STEER A STEADY COURSE: DURING MEETINGS.**

NOTES:

NOTES:

Steer a Steady Course: During Meetings

Step Three

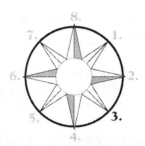

Introduction

Please continue using the Ship's Wheel diagram (from Step Two) to apply the methods of three more sections (between the spokes) in your meetings:

Provide a Context

Use a Consent Agenda

Add Process to Content and Topics

You'll also have a template for taking brief meeting notes to create an official meeting record.

Providing a context includes making sure all information that could have an impact on the meeting is shared early in the meeting. This prevents working on issues that may have changed since you last met.

Using a Consent Agenda (sometimes called a consent calendar) is a way to save time on routine items that need consent but don't require group discussion.

Adding processes (techniques or methods) to content (topics to discuss) introduces you to ways of moving more quickly through the predictable three stages of a discussion: Open, Narrow, and Close. Another good technique is to simplify the note taking to substitute a meeting summary for meeting minutes.

Purpose of This Step

Use this step to practice using, or become familiar with, several meeting methods, group process tools, and a note-taking template for future meetings.

Checklist of Results

By completing Step Three, you will:

☐ Set the context for the meeting as you get under way

☐ Understand the use of a Consent Agenda when discussion is unnecessary but acceptance of information for the group or approval of an action is required

☐ Understand the concept of moving a discussion through three stages: Opening, Narrowing, and Closing; and know a method for completing each stage when discussing any topic

☐ Adopt, or modify and adopt, a template for taking notes, called a Meeting Log.

Resource in *Roberta*

From *Roberta's Rules of Order,* read "Respecting Everyone's Time by Steering a Steady Course," (Chapter Seven), especially on the "Ship's Wheel" graphic, pp. 102–104; and "Streamlining Discussions with a Clear Destination," Chapter Twelve.

Information You'll Need to Use

Provide a Context ☑

This section is simple but powerful. I've seen many meetings launch into a subject before checking to see if everyone knows the same background information and is aware of events that occurred since the last meeting that may affect the decisions of the group.

For example, a business team was convened to plan a new orientation program for those just hired. The day before, the president of the organization had announced a hiring freeze until further notice. The group surely needed this information to decide whether and how to proceed.

Take a few moments to bring everyone up to date on recent information that could have an impact on decisions at your meeting.

Use a Consent Agenda ☑

This is a quick (closing) technique to save time in meetings. Most regular meetings, such as of a Board of Directors or other management team, waste time discussing completed transactions. This doesn't mean these items aren't important; it's just that they don't need discussion. However, they do need a vote of acceptance or approval (close). Items of this sort are grouped together into a "consent agenda".

These could also be things that have been completed by staff or others, but the group needs to know about, such as renewal of a contract, lease, etc. It could also be a vote taken by e-mail that needs to be officially acknowledged in the meeting record.

Items on the consent agenda (committee, team, or officer reports; financial reports, etc.) should be sent within the full agenda to members prior to the meeting via e-mail.

At the meeting any item on the consent agenda portion of the agenda can be "moved" from this category and made a topic for discussion by the request of any member. It's important that this technique **not** be used to "railroad" a decision that needs to go through all three phases of discussion in the group.

Add Process Tools to the Topics ☑

A meeting always has two things (or more) happening at once: the content or **what topics** are being discussed, and the process or **how the group is approaching each topic.** Think of the content being one side of the coin, say heads, and the process being the other, or tails. They are inseparable, joined together and always present. Most meetings focus on the content and forget the process, until a discussion breaks down.

A respected colleague once told me that *discuss* is a dangerous word to have on an agenda! This is because the discussion of any topic can go in many directions or tangents without coming to a conclusion. Discussion can also become a win-lose debate or heated exchange. Sometimes groups get stuck in endless brainstorming.

What follows is a simple three-step process developed by a firm named Interaction Associates, called "Open, Narrow, and Close." All discussions need to go through these three stages to reach a conclusion.

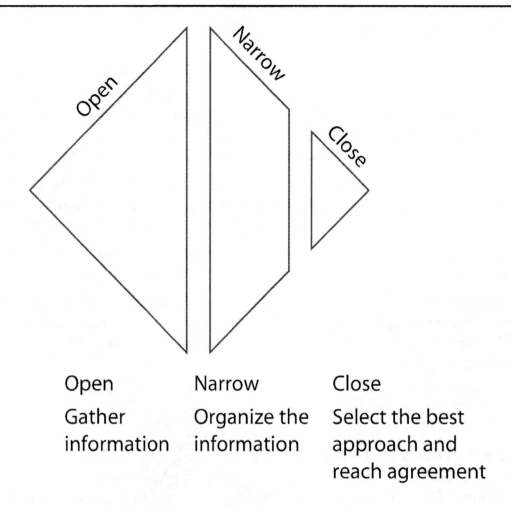

Open	Narrow	Close
Gather information	Organize the information	Select the best approach and reach agreement

Source: copyright Interaction Associates. Reproduced with permission.

Using another image, think of a funnel that you pour liquid into. The top is larger than the rest (Opening). As the liquid goes down, it hits the narrow channel (Narrowing) before it comes out the bottom (Closing).

If there is too much coming in too fast in the opening, it may overflow and never get through. This illustrates that it's often important go more slowly at first, and to gain momentum later. This suggestion also comes from Interaction Associates.

Most groups know how to open well, using brainstorming. The harder tasks are to narrow (analyze and prioritize) and close by reaching an agreement. Step Three gives you some tools and techniques for Open, Narrow, and Close, all developed by Interaction Associates.

Techniques for Discussing a Topic as a Group

Opening

Gather information. Here are two options for brainstorming:

Option A

Guidelines for brainstorming *verbally as a group:*

- Set a time limit (start with five minutes, and expand if needed).
- Write ideas on large flipchart paper posted on the wall.
- Generate ideas without discussing.
- Build on ideas of others.
- Avoid criticism or evaluation.

Option B

Guidelines for brainstorming *silently as individuals:*

- Write down your ideas.
- Compare your list with those of one or two others.
- Generate sticky notes, one idea per sticky.
- Write clearly in large letters (use watercolor markers).
- Post on flipchart paper on the wall.

Narrowing

- Clarify what is on the list or stickies.
- Discard duplicates.
- Sort by category (and name the category).

- Prioritize by selecting the top five (or one-third of the list) regardless of the categories. Decide on criteria (such as most urgent, most important, most impact).

- Use sticky dots or stars to indicate choices.

- Count the dots or stars in each category.

- Discuss preferences and decide highest category and highest options.

- Other:

Closing

Agree on additional criteria or constraints against which to evaluate choices. Decide on criteria (such as how much cost, personnel, time, etc.).

Examples:

Will this decision cost more than _____ dollars? (set a limit)

Will this decision require hiring people? _____ (yes or no?)

Will this decision take more than _____ time? (set a limit)

Others:

_____

_____

Compare your options against the criteria. You will want to select a solution that meets the most criteria.

Consider multiple answers (both this and that) and combine alternatives.

For Less Complex Decisions

Ask for someone to state a short verbal proposal, then take a multiple choice "straw poll" to get an indication of the current level of support using the five levels of Gradients of Agreement, as explained in Step Four. Check for agreement, state a verbal motion and vote.

For More Complex Decisions

For more complex decisions, complete a written proposal (see Step Four) and use the Gradients of Agreement (also Step Four) to modify it before voting on a motion.

A Template for a Meeting Record or "Log" (Minutes)

Name of the group:

_____

Date of the meeting: _____

Those who attended: _____

What we planned to accomplish (here, insert the list of meeting outcomes from the agenda):

_____

_____

Decisions that were made: _____

_____

Information needed to understand decisions:

_____

_____

Follow-up action items (see attached Action Plan):

Topics to add to the next meeting's agenda:

_____

Next meeting:

    Date and location:

    _____

    Leader: _____

    Timekeeper: _____

    Notetaker: _____

    Egalitarian: _____

What to read or do to be prepared:

_____

_____

Agenda for Step Three

Sections	Method or Directions	Estimated Time
Transition Start the meeting	Refreshments and conversation Rotate roles	15–30 min.
Roles Purpose Courtesy Guidelines	Facilitator: review purpose, meeting checklist and remind the group of the Courtesy Guidelines	5–10 min.
Introduction and material Agenda The Meeting Wheel	Read aloud together Review the full agenda; adjust times as needed Review Step Two	5–10 min.
Provide a context	Complete #1 in Step Three Worksheet	10–15 min.
Consent agenda	Complete #2	10–15 min.
Add process to content: Open, Narrow, Close	Complete #3	20–30 min.
Write a meeting summary	Complete #4	5–10 min.
Reflect	Complete #5	5–10 min.
Conclude	Complete #6	5–10 min.

Step Three Worksheet

1. Provide a Context for This Meeting

- What has occurred since we met that everyone needs to know?

  _____

2. Use a Consent Agenda

- What have we accomplished so far that we need to "ratify" as a group? (Example: review and confirm use of the courtesy guidelines and the meeting plan.)

  _____

3. Add Process to Content

- Discuss a topic (content) that is important to your group's work. Complete the three stages of Open, Narrow, and Close using the techniques (process) suggested.

  Topic: _____

- Open: _____

- Narrow: _____

- Close: _____

4. Keep a Meeting Record

Review the Meeting Record or "Log" (Minutes) and decide what you want to use for your future meetings. (Modify this template until it works well for your group.)

5. Reflect

How did we do?

1. What worked well when applying these techniques? _____

2. What didn't work as well? _____

3. When we discussed a topic using Open, Narrow, and Close, what did we learn?

   _____

4. What improvements can we make in our future meetings? (Reach agreement)

   _____

6. Conclude

- Wrap up. Are there any actions to complete to follow up on this meeting?

What to Do	By Whom	By When

- Return to the Checklist of Results at the beginning of this section and check all items.

- Who will take this role at the next meeting?

  Leader _____ Timekeeper _____

  Egalitarian _____ Notetaker _____

- What do we need to do to prepare for the next step?

From *Roberta's Rules of Order*, please read Chapter Three, "Developing Proposals Before Launching Motions," pages 33–46.

YOU'VE COMPLETED STEP THREE. NOW GO TO STEP FOUR, **PREPARE A PROPOSAL FOR ACTION WITH A MOTION.**

Prepare a Proposal for Action with a Motion

Step Four

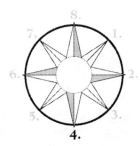

Introduction

One of the key difficulties with "motions" in a meeting is the timing. Some parliamentary meeting methods require that a motion be made before a group can discuss the issue. This sequence creates a problem.

If a motion is a method to move forward, why do groups get stuck? A motion is a committee's or someone's "solution"—but a solution to what problem or opportunity? What other possible solutions are there? Once a motion is on the table, people become polarized into supporting or opposing the motion. This doesn't help solve problems creatively.

According to Interaction Associates, a *problem* is merely a *situation* that someone (or a group) would like to change. It may be a problem to some, and not others. If something is to change, the group must be in agreement on the problem first. (There can also be opportunities for improvement that require a change.) Separating and clarifying the problem or opportunity from the possible solutions is essential before making a motion. Then you can develop a proposal that includes more information and ends with a recommendation or motion.

After presenting a proposal, it is often helpful to get feedback and modify it. In *Roberta's Rules of Order* there are no "amendments"—only modifications or improvements that the group agrees upon following, a structured discussion (using the process Open, Narrow and Close, covered in Step Three).

There are many ways to do this. One is a five-response method called Gradients of Agreement developed by Sam Kaner and colleagues at Community at Work. After this Step, your group will be able to use this method in your meetings to improve proposals and motions.

Purpose of This Step

This step gives you a method for preparing a short proposal that addresses the situation (problem or opportunity) before presenting a solution (which is often the same as a motion).

Checklist of Results

By completing Step Four, you will:

☐ Use a diagram to illustrate a successful sequence for problem solving or opportunity seeking

☐ Explore several ways to present a proposal that concludes with a motion, and modify a template for proposal making to fit your organization

☐ Understand the steps in using the Gradients of Agreement that show the levels of support for a proposal or motion

Resource in *Roberta*

From *Roberta's Rules of Order,* please read Chapter Three, "Developing Proposals Before Launching Motions," pages 33–46.

Information You'll Need to Use

In quality improvement methods worldwide, there are procedures to follow when solving a problem. Every source recommends understanding the problem and its causes before seeking solutions. (There is often more than one solution to a problem.)

If you face a new opportunity rather than a vexing problem, it's important to know why this opportunity exists. According to Interaction Associates, if you can't get agreement on the problem or opportunity, you probably won't get agreement on the solution.

Options for Developing a Proposal

There are several ways develop a proposal for action. Any proposal to be voted upon should be circulated to board members in advance.

Proposal for Action: Option A

The Problem or Opportunity:

1. The facts (the situation is . . .)

2. The cost or impact (this costs or affects us in these ways . . .)

3. Main causes (the situation exists because . . .)

The Solution (or Multiple Solutions)

4. Conditions for success (a solution needs to include . . .)

5. Options and best practices considered (several options are . . .)

6. Recommended solution (the motion), based on 1 through 5 (We move that . . .)

The Implementation Plan

7. Suggested action plan (If approved, this is what will need to be implemented . . .)

Proposal for Action: Option B

A. **Background:** context and brief history of the situation

B. **Situation:** factual statement of situation and causes

C. **Analysis:** alternatives considered and criteria used

D. **Cost:** statement of funding needed or budget (attach)

E. **Time:** estimated timeline for implementation

F. **People:** the person or team who will implement

G. **The Motion:** one or two sentences stating the recommended change

Gradients of Agreement

Sam Kaner and colleagues at Community at Work have developed a method for testing the waters, or taking a straw poll, called Gradients of Agreement. This is a process that allows everyone to respond to a proposal or idea with one of five choices.

Level	Response	Sample Statement
5	Enthusiasm	I endorse it enthusiastically
4	Cautious support	I support it with minor reservations
3	Ambivalent support	I have mixed feelings
2	Little support	I don't like it
1	No support	I can't actively support it
0	Stand aside	I don't like it but won't stand in the way

How to Use This Method

There are several options for using this method. You can read about it in *Roberta's Rules of Order,* page 69. The easiest method is to ask everyone to pick a number and say why he or she chose it.

Once you know the "spread" of the numbers, the leader can ask those at a level three or below (without pressuring them), "What would it take to make this proposal a four or five for you?" This information can be used to find a way to modify the proposal. Once it's been modified, check again to see if the whole group can support the changes.

If YES, then you have a general agreement and the basis for a motion to finalize the decision. If NO, then keep asking the question until you are able to reach an agreement and craft a motion to "close" on a decision.

Agenda for Step Four

Sections	Method or Directions	Estimated Time
Transition	Refreshments and conversation	15–30 min.
Start the meeting	Answer questions in #1 of Step Four Worksheet	1 min.
Purpose, intended results	Review purpose and meeting checklist	
Agenda	Review and agree or modify	5–10 min.
	Review the full agenda; adjust times as needed	
	Review as reminder	
Courtesy Guidelines		
Introduction and materials	Read the material aloud	10–15 min.
Situation before solution	Complete #2	
Preparing a proposal template: Option A, Option B	Complete #3	10–15 min.
Responding to a proposal	Complete #4	10–15 min.
Reflect	Complete #5	5–10 min.
Conclude	Complete item #6	5–10 min.

Step Four Worksheet

1. Sharing the Roles

- Who will be the next leader to guide the group in this meeting? _____
- Who will watch the time? _____
- Who will take notes? _____
- Who will be the egalitarian? _____

2. Problem or Solution?

- When someone says, "We need to hire an office manager," is that a problem or a solution? _____

- Hiring someone is a solution—but what's the problem or the situation? Perhaps the problem is that work isn't getting accomplished in time. Or it may be that (complete the sentence as you see fit): _____
_____

- Hiring an office manager may help the problem, but what else could also help, or be another solution? _____
_____

- Many times, problems and situations are "solved" but nothing changes. What's missing? _____
_____

3. Preparing a Structured Proposal

- Select a real situation that you would like to change. Use Option A or Option B to develop a one-page proposal. (Try dividing your group into two teams, each working on a different proposal. Then compare them for ease of use, Option A or B, and quality of information.)

4. Group Response to a Proposal

- Using any proposal as an example, apply the Gradients of Agreement. Ask each person to select a number that corresponds to level of support for the proposal, and say why. (You don't need to close, or reach agreement this time.)

5. Reflection

- This is Step Four of eight to apply Roberta in your group. At this midpoint, how would each of you say you are doing on these scales? (1 = poor; 5 = excellent)

  Getting through the material within about an hour for each session?

  1   2   3   4   5

  Understanding the reason behind the methods?

1   2   3   4   5

Listening to one another?

1   2   3   4   5

Learning as you go and finding it easier?

1   2   3   4   5

Having any fun?

1   2   3   4   5

The best possible individual score is 25. What's your score? _____.
The best possible group score is 25 times the number of group members
(_____ # members x 25 = _____).
How well are you doing as a group? _____
What are proud of? _____
What are you sorry about? _____
What will you either continue or change in the remaining steps?

_____

_____

6. Conclude

- Wrap up. Are there any actions to complete to follow up on this meeting?

What to Do	By Whom	By When

- Return to the Checklist of Results at the beginning of this section and check all items.

- Who will take these roles at the next meeting?

Leader _____   Timekeeper _____

Egalitarian: _____   Notetaker:_____

- What do we need to read or do in advance to prepare?

From *Roberta's Rules of Order*, read Chapter Four, "Testing the Current Before Heading for Consensus," pages 47–60, and Chapter Eleven, "Tacking Away from Debate Toward Dialogue," pages 159–170.

YOU'VE COMPLETED STEP FOUR AND YOU'RE HALFWAY THROUGH! NOW GO TO STEP FIVE, **MAKE A DECISION AS A GROUP: TACK ONE—CONSENSUS.**

Make Decisions as a Group:

Tack One—Consensus

Step Five

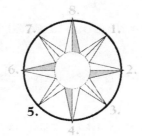

Introduction

Since the mid-1980s, there has been a trend in groups to use consensus decision making. The Japanese and the quality improvement movement in the United States were influences; however, we learned that it's not always a good fit for every culture.

Consensus is easier to reach in an organization that has strong religious or humanistic values. In smaller groups, it comes more easily when there is little controversy or the situation isn't complex. Step Five gives you a method to determine when to use consensus and when to avoid it.

Consensus can also bring an organization to a halt (in nautical terms, "becalmed") if *everyone* has to agree on *everything*. A few uncompromising people can become the minority that rules. Sometimes, in an effort to get everyone on board, a consensus decision ends up so watered down that it is a poor decision.

In using consensus, each group needs to have a step-by-step procedure that can be written down ("this is how we do it") and repeated with predictable consistency. You'll have a chance to practice this in Step Five.

It's also important to decide on a bail-out plan, in case you start to sink. What method will you use if there isn't enough time or energy, or if the situation is highly complex or controversial?

Purpose of This Step

Step Five gives you tools to assess the appropriateness of using consensus, and a process to do it well if you choose it as a decision-making method.

Checklist of Results

By completing Step Five, you will:

☐ Define consensus for your group

☐ Use a decision-making "wind gauge" to determine the levels of controversy and complexity

☐ Learn six factors to consider before using consensus, and complete your group's profile

☐ Understand and use a recommended process to reach consensus

Resource in *Roberta*

From *Roberta's Rules of Order*, read Chapter Four, "Testing the Current Before Heading for Consensus," pages 47–60, and Chapter Eleven, "Tacking Away from Debate Toward Dialogue," pages 159–170.

Information You'll Need to Use

A Definition of Consensus

The generally agreed-on definition of *consensus* for group decisions is that everyone has had a chance to be heard, understands the decision, and will support its implementation (or at least will not block the group).

Consensus is not majority rule, super majority rule, or even unanimity. Consensus does not have to be used for every decision. It should also include a "bail-out" plan if consensus cannot be reached within a reasonable time.

Two Primary Forces to Consider

An organization deciding whether to use consensus as a decision-making process may need to consider a range of options and think situationally. In each situation, there are at least two primary forces to consider: the level of *controversy about* the issue and *complexity within* the issue.

Controversy means that the issue may:

- Challenge personal values or beliefs
- Put something at risk, including money or membership
- Take something away, or add something, that people feel strongly about
- Involve a change that challenges "the way things have always been done"

Complexity means that the issue may:

- Involve multiple organizational partners
- Be difficult to structure as a win-win solution
- Include the need for legal advice
- Affect the bylaws or organization's current mission

As the levels of controversy and complexity increase, so does the difficulty of reaching consensus (see the diagram that follows).

Think of the combination of controversy and complexity as four levels of wind speed, based on the "Beaufort Scale" that measures the intensity of wind. This scale was developed by a British admiral in 1805, and is still used today, to help sailors observe and estimate the strength of the winds around them:

1. Calm air
2. Moderate breeze
3. Gale winds
4. Hurricane

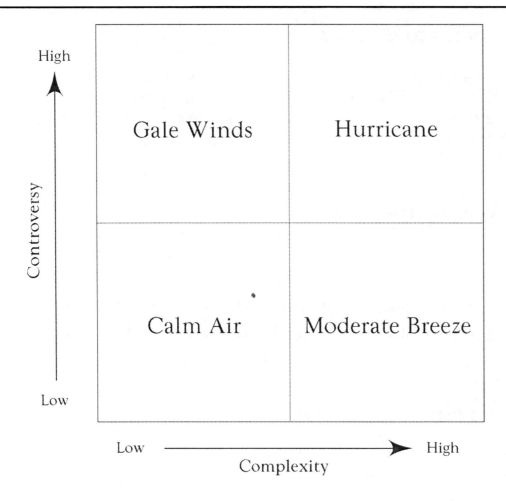

Consensus is easy to reach when there is calm air. Even the moderate breezes of increased complexity can be overcome.

However, if the storm in your meeting grows stronger, as when there is an increase in the level of controversy, gale winds will make it hard to reach an agreement by consensus. When there is both complexity and controversy at full force, you have a hurricane. It is almost impossible to reach consensus in this situation.

This is why it makes sense to set a time limit to reconsider reaching consensus. Striving for consensus is admirable; collapsing from it is unnecessary. A backup plan, such as a predetermined level of concordance (a substantial majority), would be a way to move forward.

Other Factors to Consider

There are at least six other factors to consider in deciding whether to use consensus decision making:

1. *Size* of the group making the decision

2. *Time* you have available to make the decision, and the urgency of making it

3. *Support* that you need (buy-in) to implement the decision

4. *Values* related to inclusion of all stakeholders

5. *Amount of trust* and experience working together as a group

6. *Consensus track record* of past success, often related to culture

	A	B	C
Size of group	Small (1–5)	Medium (15–50)	Large (50–100+)
Time, urgency	Unlimited	Not rushed	Short
Support (buy-in) needed	High	Some	Not much
Shared values	Strong	Mixed	Weak
Trust	High	Moderate	Low
Consensus track record	Excellent	Good	Poor

A Process for Striving for Consensus

Begin with Four Agreements

- Agree on a common definition of consensus.

- Agree on expectations for courteous behavior during dialogue (use courtesy guidelines and add to them, if necessary).

- Agree on a time limit for this decision; how long is too long to strive to reach consensus?

- Agree on the process to be used (see below).

Stage One

- Present the proposal or issue (as a handout or written on flipcharts).

- Encourage questions for understanding; clarify factually without promoting or defending the issue.

- Give everyone an opportunity to voice his or her perspective, ask questions, and speak for or against the proposal.

- Call for consensus; if it is reached, stop here and restate the agreement.

Next Stages, If Needed

If you don't have an agreement, continue to stage two or three as needed. This is located in *Roberta's Rules of Order* on pages 56–57. Be prepared to use the backup voting method of concordance in Chapter Five, page 61.

Agenda for Step Five

Sections	Method or Directions	Estimated Time
Transition Start the meeting	Refreshments and conversation	15–30 min.
Roles	Answer question #1 of Step Five Worksheet	1 min.
Purpose intended results	Review purpose and meeting checklist	
Agenda	Review the full agenda; adjust times as needed	5–10 min.
Courtesy Guidelines	Review and agree or modify	
Read introduction and material	Complete #2	10–15 min.
Define consensus	Complete #3	10–15 min.
Assess controversy and complexity	Complete #4	10–15 min.
Determine group profile	Complete #5	10–15 min.
Use a process to reach consensus	Complete #6	5–10 min.
Reflect and conclude	Complete #7 and #8	5–10 min.

Step Five Worksheet

Please complete these questions or directions.

1. **Sharing the Roles**

   - Who will lead this meeting? _____

   - Who will watch the time? _____

   - Who will take notes, if needed? _____

   - Who will help balance the participation? _____

2. **Read the Material Aloud**

   - Rotate reading sections.

3. **Define Consensus**

   - Agree on the definition you'll use: _____

4. **Assess Controversy and Complexity**

   - What decisions do you tend to make as a group? _____
     _____

   - Where do they fall on the scale of complexity? _____

     Scale of controversy? _____

   - List several decisions that you will need to make in the future. _____
     _____
     _____

   - Plot them on the box of the complexity-controversy figure, using the four-point Beaufort scale: (1) calm, (2) moderate breeze, (3) gale, (4) hurricane.

   - Which are level one and two on the Beaufort Scale, meaning decisions easily made by consensus?

   - Which are level three or four and may need another method of decision making? Mark them accordingly.

5. **Determine Group Profile**

   - Using the factors to consider that are described in this step and the chart (see "Other Factors to Consider"), circle those that apply to your group.

   - Do these circles fall primarily in column A, B, or C? _____

   - If these circles are primarily in column A, it will be easier for your group to reach consensus regardless of controversy or complexity.

   - If the circles are primarily in column B, you'll have about a fifty-fifty chance.

- If the circles are primarily in column C, consensus may be possible but difficult.

- Given the profile of this group and other factors, do you plan to use consensus as your primary method of decision making? If so, please use the process for striving for consensus outlined in this step.

- Practice using it on a real problem. Try stating the problem, beginning with "We need to decide how to . . ." or use another way of stating a problem ("We need to decide whether or not to . . .").

6. Strive for Consensus

- For the desired decision you have just stated, use the consensus process seen above and check off each step as you complete it.

7. Reflection

- What is your decision? _____

- How well did the process work? _____

- What would you improve next time, and how? _____

8. Conclude

- Wrap up. Are there any actions to complete to follow up on this meeting?

What to Do	By Whom	By When

- Return to the Checklist of Results at the beginning of this section and check all items.

- Who will take these roles at the next meeting?

  Leader _____ Timekeeper _____

  Egalitarian_____ Notetaker _____

- What do we need to read or do in advance to prepare?

From *Roberta's Rules of Order*, read Chapter Five, "Reaching for Concordance When Consensus Is an Obstacle," pages 61–76.

YOU'VE COMPLETED STEP FIVE; NOW GO TO STEP SIX, **MAKE A DECISION AS A GROUP: TACK TWO—CONCORDANCE.**

NOTES:

Make Decisions as a Group:

Tack Two—Concordance

Step Six

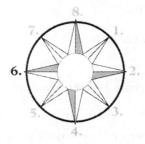

Introduction

The previous step outlined a method for using consensus for making group decisions—when it is appropriate. Some groups aren't comfortable using consensus as a decision-making method because it can potentially keep a group from making a decision in a short time period.

Consensus can also result in a decision everyone agrees to but is so watered down that no one really feels good about it or cares about implementation. People are generally motivated by what they care about. Without caring, the commitment to implement can lack luster, like a dull brass bell.

Striving for consensus, by using guidelines for dialogue and listening, is worthwhile. However, being unable to make a decision because one or a few people are unwilling to go along can result in minority rule. Groups need a backup plan when using consensus, such as a form of voting.

After working hard to reach consensus and falling short, some groups don't want to resort to the rule of a simple majority. They would rather use a super majority (also known as "substantial majority") rule called *concordance*. This section explains the differences, the terminology, and how to use concordance.

Purpose of This Step

To be able to make a wise decision, based on your organization's culture, as to whether and how to use a decision-making method called Concordance.

Checklist of Results

By completing Step Six, you will:

☐ Understand the differences among consensus, concordance, and conventional majority rule.

☐ Be able to use this information to decide which method will work best for your group.

☐ Apply another method for reflecting on your effectiveness during these training sessions, and in your future meetings.

Resource in *Roberta*

From *Roberta's Rules of Order*, read Chapter Five, "Reaching for Concordance When Consensus Is an Obstacle," pages 61–76.

Information You'll Need to Use

The Middle Ground Between Simple Majority Rule and Consensus

In most situations, Roberta's Rules for Meetings encourages seeking a middle ground between consensus and simple majority rule. One option is to reach a super majority, also called substantial agreement or "concordance." This is defined as 75% (or more) of those voting, given the presence of a quorum, to approve a proposal.

The goal of consensus is for everyone to support the implementation of the proposal. Although a group may strive for consensus, reaching substantial agreement or concordance may be a reasonable result when the group is working within a stated time limit.

The group decides on its own desired level of substantial agreement, or concordance, from 75 to 90%. This is written into the group's customized Rules for Meetings (see Step Eight and example in the Resources).

Types of Majority Options for Decisions

Concepts of majority can be summarized by the percentage each one represents:

- **Simple majority**   50% plus one (over half, with a quorum)

- **Super majority**   Usually 66% (two-thirds), but more than 50% plus one

- **Substantial majority**   75% or more

- **Unanimous**   100%

A way to illustrate this is to visualize the face of an analog clock. Assuming a board of twelve members and in terms of hours alone, a simple majority is anything at or beyond 7:00 (or 50% plus one hour). A super majority would be from 7:00 to 12:00 with, a substantial majority beginning at about 9:00 and continuing up to 12:00. Unanimous is at 12:00.

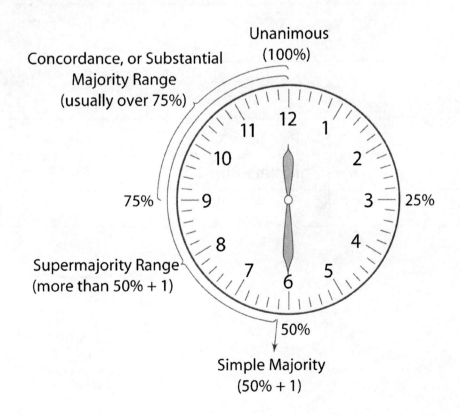

Agenda for Step Six

Sections	Method or Directions	Estimated Time
Transition	Refreshments and conversation	15–30 min.
Start the meeting Purpose	Rotate roles	1 min.
Checklist of results	Leader: review purpose and meeting checklist	5–10 min.
Agenda	Review the full agenda; adjust times as needed	5–10 min.
Courtesy Guidelines	Review and agree or modify	
Rotate Roles	Complete item #1 in Step Six Worksheet	10–15 min.
Read material aloud	Complete #2	
Decision making using concordance	Complete #3	10–15 min.
Evaluate use of concordance	Complete #4	10–15 min.
Reflect	Complete #5	10–15 min.
Conclude	Complete #6	10–15 min.

Step Six Worksheet

Please complete these questions or directions.

1. Sharing the Roles

- Who will be the next leader to guide the group in this meeting? _____
- Who will watch the time? _____
- Who will take notes, if needed? _____
- Who will help us balance participation? _____

2. Read the Material Aloud

- What is the difference between a simple majority and a super majority?
- What does substantial agreement mean?
- If we choose not to use a simple majority, what level of substantial majority (concordance) do we feel comfortable with for a backup voting plan? _____

3. Try Using Concordance for a Decision

- Select an actual decision that your group needs to make to try using concordance. For this exercise, assume that concordance is a super majority of 80% of the group; for a group of ten people, eight of you would need to agree.
- Discuss your options using methods to open and narrow. Close by using the decision-making level you have chosen.

    We need to decide how we can (or whether to) . . .

    Open: _____

    Narrow: _____

    Close: _____

4. Evaluate Your Experience

- What worked well using this method? _____
- What didn't work well? _____
- Do we feel comfortable using concordance as a backup voting method? _____

5. Learning from Reflection

- Using the triangle of Results, Process, and Relationships, answer these questions:
- How is our balance among these three elements?

    _____

- What do we need to do to be in better balance?

    _____

6. Conclude

- Wrap up. Are there any actions to complete to follow up on this meeting?

What to Do	By Whom	By When

- Return to the Checklist of Results at the beginning of this section and check all items.
- Who will take these roles at the next meeting?

  Leader _____ Timekeeper _____

  Egalitarian_____ Notetaker_____

- What do we need to read or do in advance to prepare? _____

From *Roberta's Rules of Order,* please read Chapter Eight, "Ending with Reflection and an Eye on the Horizon," pages 115–127.

YOU'VE COMPLETED STEP SIX; NOW GO TO STEP SEVEN, **TIE THINGS UP AT THE END OF A MEETING.** YOU'RE ALMOST DONE!

Tie Things up: Ending Meetings

Step Seven

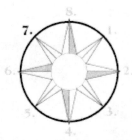

Introduction

This step returns to the Ship's Wheel seen in Step Two to apply the methods of the final three spokes in your meetings: continue the momentum, conclude with reflection, and complete an expanded agenda.

Continue the momentum means to make a plan about how to follow through on the work that was done in this meeting. The best tool to use is an Action Plan. To see the results of the meeting, you can return to the Checklist of intended results that was filled in at the beginning of the meeting and check off what was completed.

Conclude with reflection involves using one of several means of thinking about the meeting and learning from this experience. You've already leaned to make a divided list of what worked well on one side of the vertical line and "what needs work" before the next meeting on the other side. This step gives you another option.

Complete an expanded agenda means to draft the meeting Checklist of intended results for the next meeting and the beginnings of an agenda.

Purpose of This Step

In this step you will become familiar with, and practice using, several more tools to wrap things up at the end of the meeting. They include planning the next steps, and learning from the experience of the meeting how to improve your next one as you develop the next meeting's agenda.

Checklist of Results

By completing Step Seven, you will:

☐ Summarize the meeting results and use the Checklist of Results to gauge how much you accomplished.

☐ Review and expand the Action Plan template we're already familiar with.

☐ Use several tools to pause and reflect on the meeting's results and process; you will also consider how well the group worked together and the benefit (if any) to the members' relationships.

☐ Develop the Checklist of intended results for your next meeting.

☐ Decide on an agenda format and complete a draft for your next meeting.

Resource in *Roberta*

From *Roberta's Rules of Order,* please read Chapter Eight, "Ending with Reflection and an Eye on the Horizon," pages 115–127.

Information You'll Need to Use

These techniques refer back to the Ship's Wheel and will help you tie up loose ends as you finish a meeting.

Continue the Momentum ☑

Summarize the Meeting Content

At the end of the meeting, the leader (or another designated person) should make a short verbal summary of the progress that's been made. This is about the meeting's content or topics. It could also be done during the meeting to help keep the group focused and motivated. Review the Meeting Checklist.

At the end of the meeting, reviewing the Checklist of intended results is a good way to know what's been completed and what needs to be continued at another meeting, or assigned to a team.

Complete the Action Plan

An Action Plan can be used during the meeting as specific follow-up actions are suggested and agreed to. Writing down the task and the person to do it may be enough until the end of the meeting; at that time the Action Plan can be added to and reviewed as a complete list, with time limits assigned for each task. A report on progress should be included in the next meeting's agenda.

Conclude with Reflection ☑

Interaction Associates has developed a model for measuring the success of a work group, whether in one meeting or over time. It depicts three equally weighted elements of success: results, process and relationships.

When groups achieve results at the expense of relationships or a healthy group process, people can suffer "burnout" or become demotivated. An overemphasis on relationships or process, without accomplishing anything significant (results), can also be demotivating. Balancing the three elements is the goal.

The triangle on the next page shows the three dimensions and key areas to assess.

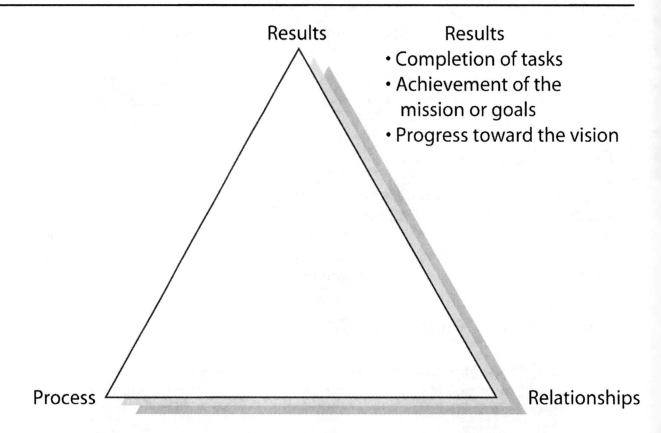

Results
- Completion of tasks
- Achievement of the mission or goals
- Progress toward the vision

Process
- How the work gets done
- How the work is planned and managed
- How the work is evaluated

Relationships
- How people treat each other
- Whether people feel respected and valued
- How people feel about their contribution

Source: Copyright Interaction Associates. Reproduced with permission.

Complete an Expanded Agenda ☑

Chart the Course for the Next Meeting

It may seem "out of order" to focus on planning an agenda in the step about "tying things up" at the end of a meeting, but the end of a meeting is the BEST time to think about and plan the next meeting. Review your list of any deferred items, consider the feedback about the current meeting and complete the following.

List Your Intended Results

The first thing to do when planning a meeting is to make a short list of what you intend and hope to accomplish—the meeting Checklist. It should state each item in concrete terms.

One way to begin is to ask, "When we end this meeting, what do we need to have decided or made progress on? What would make us feel good about having this meeting?" Look at the meeting Checklists in each step of this Guide for examples.

Select an Agenda Format

Once you have established what you want to get done (Checklist of Results), look at the list. Are there items that you need to Open, Narrow, or Close, or all three? Consider how much time each process, such as brainstorming, prioritizing, etc., will take and how much time you have to work with. Some take more time than others. Enter all the things you have learned to do at the beginning and end of the meeting in the first and last boxes, and list the topics covered to get these results, along with their processes, in separate boxes. Fill in the timeframe in minutes, and add them all up.

Please see the example agendas of "before and after" Roberta's Rules on the next few pages. Following the examples are several templates to use when planning your own agendas. One is in a "grid" format that has been used in this Guide (Option A). The other is a similar format without the "grid" (Option B). If these don't "fit" your group, develop a template that works for you and use it consistently.

Agenda Examples: Before and After Roberta

Before Roberta: Example of a Traditional Agenda

Maritime Institute Board Meeting

Remembering a special person - a tribute

Special reports

- Ambassadors International Exchange Project

- Tall Ships events for the coming year

- Ports and Coastal Conservancy

- Ship invitations

- Minutes: Additions, corrections, approval (previously e-mailed)

Financial report

Audit

Ships account

Budget vs. actual summary

Bridges program

- Beyond the Bell program

New budget - first draft

- Construction loan

- Status Reports:

    Ships that need repair

    Fund development

    High school summer interns

    Board planning

    Manager position - proposal 2nd draft

After Roberta: Example of an Agenda *Using the Grid Format*

Maritime Institute Board Meeting

Mission

We use sail training to give youths real-life challenges that develop knowledge, skills, and attitudes needed to live healthy, productive lives.

Checklist of Results

By the end of this meeting we need to:

☐ Be informed about financial status (budget vs. actual)

☐ Decide on level of financial review this year and expedite the audit for next year

☐ Decide who will draft the new budget for board review at next meeting

☐ Get updated on fund development and kick-start grant-seeking effort

Topic (What)	Method (How)	Who	Estimated Time
Convene the meeting		Jane	9:00 a.m.
Mission or purpose	Review		10 min.
Results checklist	Is everyone clear?		
Roles: rotate			
Courtesy guidelines	Do we agree to follow them?		
Connect everyone	Quick check-in Remembering a special person - a tribute	All (30 sec. each) Jane	15 min.
Context update	Special reports: • Ambassadors international • Ship reception invitations	Mark	20 min.

Topic (What)	Method (How)	Who	Estimated Time
Consent agenda (routine items)	No discussion needed: Change or approve minutes Routine reports	Jane	10 min.
Content topics	Financial update: • Audit • Ship's account • Finance: budget and fund development • Programs: interns, etc Status updates: (for clarification only) • Tall Ships events • Ports and Coastal Conservancy • Ship's maintenance	Paul Mark Judy	20 min. 10 min.
Continue	Board planning: • Summarize notes • Next steps, action plan • Manager position proposal	Joyce	20 min.
Conclude	Summarize and reflect Follow up Next meeting date and time	All	10 min. end 10:30 a.m.

The following are two options (templates) to customize and use when planning an agenda. Option A looks like the "grid" format above. For those who don't like this format, use the more traditional format without lines, Option B.

Option A: Template for Charting an Agenda

Meeting: _____ Location: _____

Date: _____ Time: _____

Mission or specific purpose:

_____

_____

Meeting Checklist of intended results: By the end of this meeting we will:

☐

☐

☐

Topic (What)	Method (How)	Who	Est. Time
Convene Mission or purpose Intended results Roles (Timekeeper, etc.) Decision-making option Courtesy Guidelines	Refreshments and conversation Review roles Is everyone clear? Do we agree to follow?		
Connect	Quick check-in (What's new? What's on your mind?)		
Context	What's happened since we met?		

Topic (What)	Method (How)	Who	Est. Time
Consent	What's routine that we need to complete?		
Content	Topics with process to Open (brainstorm), Narrow (prioritize), Close (decide)		
Continue	What will we need to continue (do next)?		
Conclude	Summarize and reflect		

Tips

- Allow at least fifteen minutes for transitioning into the meeting. Food always helps, but allow time to eat before starting.

- Allow at least ten minutes at the beginning and end to convene and conclude.

- Put in one topic per "box"; add the processes: Open, Narrow, or Close.

- Allow enough time to work through the process, given the group's size. Write the time limit in each box in minutes ("15"), not clock time. (Use clock time at the beginning, and midway for a benchmark.)

- Show when the meeting is scheduled to end. If the group is running late, ask permission to add time to an agenda.

- Try to keep evening meetings to two hours and conclude by 9:00 p.m.

- Keep your Courtesy Guidelines visible, and review them regularly.

Option B: Template for Charting an Agenda

Meeting: _____ Location: _____
Date: _____ Time: _____

Mission or Specific Purpose:

_____

_____

Meeting Checklist of Intended Results:

By the end of this meeting we will:

☐

☐

☐

Sections and Topics	*Process*	*Person*	*Time*
Convene			
Connect			
Context			
Consent			
Content			
Continue			
Conclude			

Agenda for Step Seven

Sections	Method or Directions	Estimated Time
Transitioning	Refreshments and conversation	15–30 min.
Starting the meeting	Rotate roles	5–10 min.
Roles		
Purpose	Review purpose and meeting checklist; remind the group of courtesy guidelines	5–10 min.
Checklist of Results		
Courtesy Guidelines		
Agenda	Review the full agenda; adjust times as needed	
Read information provided aloud	Identify specific things covered in this step	
Meeting Wheel		
Summarize the meeting	Complete item #1 in Step Seven Worksheet	10–15 min.
Review meeting checklist (intended results)	Complete #2	10–15 min.
Complete the action plan	Complete #3	20–30 min.
Conclude with reflection: results, process, and relationships	Complete #4	5–10 min.
Plan next meeting's agenda	Complete #5	5–10 min.
Conclude	Complete #6	5–10 min.

Step Seven Worksheet

Please complete these questions and directions.

1. Summarize the Meeting

- Use this opportunity to summarize what you have learned so far using this Guide.

  _____

  _____

2. Review the Meeting Checklist (Intended Results)

- Look back at the meeting Checklists for each of the training sessions. What have you completed as a group? _____

  _____

3. Complete the Action Plan

What do we need to do to follow through or complete any training before planning our meeting agenda? _____

What to Do	By Whom	By When

Who will follow up with everyone before the next meeting?_____

4. Reflect on Your Progress

- Using the triangle diagram in this step, answer these questions on using this Guide.

  Results: Are we making progress? Are we achieving results? _____

  Process: How clear are we about how we do things? Are we duplicating effort?

  _____

  Relationships: How well are we getting along? Are we listening well? supporting each other?_____

- What improvements can we make in our future sessions? (Reach agreement.)

  _____

  _____

5. Plan Our Next Meeting's Agenda

- What are the intended results for our group's actual next meeting? Develop the meeting Results Checklist.

- By the end of this meeting we will:

  ☐

  ☐

  ☐

- Complete the first draft of your next meeting's agenda (choose a format).

- Who will finish drafting the agenda for the next meeting to achieve these results?

  _____

6. Conclude

- Wrap up. Are there any actions to complete to follow up on this meeting?

What to Do	By Whom	By When

- Return to the Checklist of Results at the beginning of this section and check all items.

- Who will take these roles at the next meeting?

  Leader _____ Timekeeper _____

  Egalitarian _____ Notetaker _____

- What do we need to read or do in advance to prepare?

  Read the Introduction, pages 1–12, and Chapter Two, "Rescuing Democratic Principles from Parliamentary Procedure," pages 21–30.

YOU'VE COMPLETED STEP SEVEN; NOW GO TO THE LAST STEP, **CUSTOMIZE ROBERTA'S RULES: YOUR MEETING METHOD**.

Customize Roberta's Rules:

Your Meeting Method

Step Eight

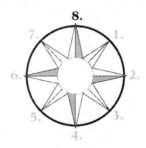

Introduction

All decision-making groups need at least a simple structure to get results. Without thinking (or on the advice of a well-meaning lawyer), nonprofits will use a parliamentary method such as Robert's Rules of Order. This isn't necessary, and it is often too constrictive for smaller groups.

According to Stephen Nill, an attorney and the founder of an organization called CharityChannel.com:

> *Anyone who has ever participated in nonprofit board meetings that were governed by Robert's Rules of Order will not be surprised to learn of the military background of its author: U.S. Army General Henry M. Robert. The rules make a good deal of sense to those who love rigid structure, and rules, rules, rules.*

> *After sitting on nonprofit boards and serving as legal counsel to nonprofit organizations for more than two decades, I have come to loathe Robert's Rules of Order. I've seen how these rules often stifle meaningful dialog and problem solving by giving advantage to some while relegating others to the sidelines. Indeed, they rarely coax a full contribution from those who are naturally quiet and thoughtful, or who hold back because of a lack of standing in society and/or within the board itself. It is this latter failing that cuts against the grain of our sector—a sector that so obviously values, and draws strength from, full participation from those of diverse views.*

This step gives you a quick way to customize and codify your organization's own "Roberta's Rules for Meetings." (Then change the name to your organization, such as ABC's Rules for Meetings.)

Purpose of This Step

This step brings the meeting and decision-making methods in this Guide into a written set of special rules for meetings that you can use consistently in your organization.

Checklist of Results

By completing Step Eight, you will:

☐ Know that many small groups assume they need parliamentary procedure, when it's most useful for large groups

☐ Customize Special Rules for Meetings for your organization to have a set of codified guidelines

☐ Select a backup method of parliamentary procedure for managing a large voting meeting

Resource in *Roberta*

Read the Introduction, pages 1–12, and Chapter Two, "Rescuing Democratic Principles from Parliamentary Procedure."

Information You'll Need to Use

If you visualize nonprofit governance in the form of a triangle, there are at least five levels each organization needs: Articles of Incorporation, Bylaws, Standing Rules or Policies, Rules for Meetings, and a Parliamentary Procedure resource.

In Robert's Rules of Order the term "Special Rules" is used to refer to how an organization makes decisions and runs its meetings. Robert's Rules of Order states that Special Rules take precedence over rules in a parliamentary resource with which they may conflict. Taking the time to customize meeting rules that everyone knows and are easy to follow will pay off!

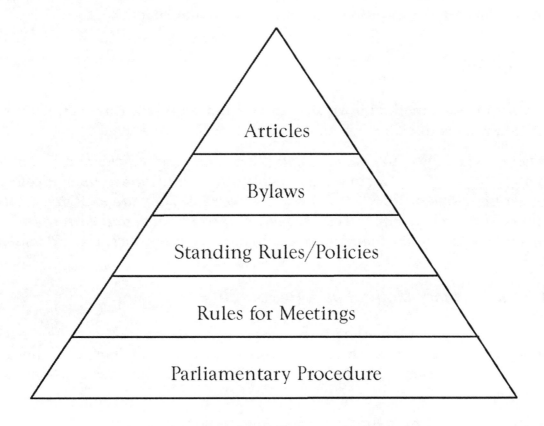

Articles

Bylaws

Standing Rules/Policies

Rules for Meetings

Parliamentary Procedure

The Governance Triangle

Specify Your Rules

According to attorney Anthony Mancuso, author of *How to Form a Nonprofit Corporation in all 50 States* from Nolo Press, you may specify the rules of order that will be used at a board of directors' meetings. The important things is to have rules or guidelines you can follow. You may also indicate any set of parliamentary procedures as your backup, particularly for a large voting meeting.

Additionally, you may specify in your bylaws a provision to add new procedures in the future by using this intentionally vague statement: "Such procedures as may be approved from time to time by the board of directors." This allows the organization some latitude to develop its own set of procedures or modify others.

Meeting Rules, once developed, require a two-thirds vote of the board to approve. After that, the designated decision-making method will take effect.

Make It Official

Stating your meeting method in your bylaws is not required. However, if your organization wishes to do so, you may add this paragraph:

The business meetings of the board, committees, and other official decision-making groups of _____ organization will be run by the agreed upon meeting rules customized from Roberta's Rules of Order, Resource A. They are kept in our official Governance Notebook along with our Articles of Incorporation and current Bylaws. For large meetings warranting more formal parliamentary procedure, we will use (select one below).

Use a Parliamentary Method as a Resource

It's a good idea to select a method of parliamentary procedure to use as a back-up method for large meetings, such as annual membership meetings, or if there is a need for a more formal structure in some high-conflict situations. Here are some available resources to choose from:

The Modern Rules of Order, American Bar Association, 2001

The Standard Code of Parliamentary Procedure, 3rd edition, by Alice Sturgis, McGraw-Hill, 1988

Robert's Rules of Order, Newly Revised 10th edition, 2000

The Complete Idiot's Guide to Robert's Rules, by Nancy Sylvester, Alpha Publications, 2004

Robert's Rules for Dummies, by C. Alan Jennings, Wiley, 2005

Roberta's Rules for Meetings

With reference to corresponding chapters in *Roberta's Rules of Order*

Rule 1: Use of Special Rules (See Roberta, Chapter Two)

A. These Rules for Meetings will be used as the regular business meeting method of the _____ organization. The rules are subordinate to (1) the organization's Bylaws, (2) the Articles of Incorporation, and (3) current state and federal laws of nonprofit public or mutual benefit organizations.

B. These rules may be further modified by concordance, or "substantial agreement," of the Board of Directors. For this organization, substantial agreement is defined as _____% majority. This does not prevent striving for consensus. Once approved, all committees, teams, and task forces within the organization will use these agreed upon rules for their business meetings.

Rule 2: Meeting Roles (See Roberta, Chapter Seven)

A. The president of the organization, or a member she or he appoints, will preside at the meeting and be called the Leader. She or he will request a volunteer Timekeeper and a Notetaker and will rotate these roles at each meeting.

B. She or he is responsible for conducting a focused meeting with the help of a designated egalitarian. The Leader will remain fair and impartial. The Leader will make the final decisions regarding the meeting content and agenda after gathering input from the group.

C. The Egalitarian will remain neutral and focus on the meeting process to help reinforce the group's agreed-on courtesy guidelines for meetings. The Leader and the Egalitarian will confer on matters of meeting process. The Egalitarian will make the final decision on the fairness of the meeting process.

D. All participants will help create and be asked to uphold the meeting courtesy guidelines. Participants will strive to reach a consensus agreement, but if it cannot be reached within _____ time, the final decision will be made by a _____% substantial majority vote, or concordance. (See options and definitions.)

E. The Notetaker will take brief notes during the meeting, on paper or flipchart. As "tangent topics" come up, she or he will make a list for future discussion. She or he will write a brief summary of the meeting and distribute it to members within _____ days (or weeks). She or he will send it electronically or by regular mail.

F. The Timekeeper will keep the Leader and the group aware of time. If the group has agreed on a specified time limit for any individual to speak, the Timekeeper will give the person a one-minute warning. At the end of the time, the person will be asked to stop. This person cannot speak again until all others have had an opportunity to speak.

G. Any group member may present a verbal or written proposal to the group for consideration. In a membership organization, a group of members (more than one person) may bring a proposal to the board.

Rule 3: Meeting Agenda (See Roberta, Chapter Seven)

A. The Leader, with suggestions from the members of the group, will draft an agenda. This will include the organization's mission at the top, the meeting purpose (if other than a regular meeting), and the meeting's checklist of intended results. The agenda will focus on accomplishing the current major strategies or goals of the organization, and accomplishing its mission.

B. In the agenda, there will a stated and expected start and end time, topics in order of priority (policy, urgency, or impact), estimated time limits in minutes for each topic, and the name of the person leading each topic.

C. Whenever possible, the agenda and other pertinent material will be distributed in advance electronically or by regular mail.

Rule 4: Quorum (See Roberta, Chapter Five)

A. A quorum is not required for holding a meeting. However, no decisions can be made that obligate the whole group without having a quorum present in person or connected electronically. For this organization, a quorum is defined as _____ members.

B. If the Leader determines that a quorum is present at the beginning of the meeting and the agenda includes items to be decided, the decision making can continue even if members leave and a quorum is no longer present.

Rule 5: Electronic Meetings and Attendance (See Roberta, Chapter Six)

A. Members who cannot conveniently attend a meeting because of distance or logistical problems may attend any meeting electronically as long as everyone can be heard clearly. A designated person will make the arrangements and the costs will be covered by _____.

B. Members who miss more than _____ meetings in person or electronically within a calendar year may be asked to resign.

C. Participants will follow the guidelines for electronic meetings found in *Roberta's Rules of Order*, starting on page 84.

Rule 6: Starting the Meeting (See Roberta, Chapter Six)

A. The tone of the meeting will be informal and friendly. Members will be given a chance to relax, with social time and food preceding the meeting to allow a fifteen-to-thirty-minute transition period.

B. There will be an opportunity in the beginning for everyone to check in briefly and update the group on any personal news, or to make announcements of interest to the group.

C. Anyone visiting the meeting will be introduced to everyone, and the group members to them, with every attempt to include them quickly.

D. If desired there may be an invocation, spiritual practice, or moment of meditation or reflection to set a positive tone.

E. Members will be given a chance to read and modify the agenda at the beginning of the meeting. The group will reach concordance before proceeding.

F. The first discussion will be about the meeting purpose, objectives, roles, expected behaviors (Courtesy Guidelines), and decision-making method for all appropriate items. The group will reach concordance before proceeding.

Rule 7: Routine Reports and Consent Agenda (See Roberta, Chapter Seven)

A. The meeting summary of the previous meeting and routine reports not requiring individual consideration will be placed on the agenda at the beginning in a "consent agenda" section. This information will be provided ahead of time or before the start of the meeting.

B. The consent agenda items will not be discussed individually unless *any* member requests that they be removed from this section and placed on the regular agenda as a separate item for discussion. The Leader will check with the group for agreement to file these reports as part of the organization's records.

Rule 8: Discussion of Issues (See Roberta, Chapters Three and Eleven)

A. Any item may be discussed that is on or added to the agenda prior to or at the beginning of the meeting. A motion or a second is not required. (Please follow the guidelines adopted by your state called the Sunshine Law, if it applies.)

B. The member(s) presenting an issue for consideration should offer it in the form of a simple (verbal) or structured (written) proposal. Written proposals should address the problem and its causes before proceeding to the solution. (See suggested structure in *Roberta's Rules of Order*, Chapter Three).

C. Whenever possible, structured proposals will be made available for members to read in advance of the meeting.

D. All members will be given an opportunity to speak or ask questions. No one member may speak a second time until all wanting to speak have spoken once.

E. When discussing a proposal, the Leader or Egalitarian will structure the discussion to proceed from opening (idea generation) to narrowing (evaluating ideas) to closing (making decisions).

F. The Leader or Egalitarian will ensure that the discussion is balanced between pros and cons and all points of view are encouraged.

G. Any member can suggest changes to a proposal. The proposal can be modified by group concordance. If the changes are not agreed on, another member may present a different proposal.

H. Up to three proposals on the same issue may be presented for consideration. If there is more than one proposal being considered, they should each be presented in writing and discussed one at a time.

Rule 9: Decision Making (See Roberta, Chapter Five)

A. All members will be given an opportunity to speak at least once on each proposal.

B. After a proposal has been presented and thoroughly discussed, the leader will ask if the group is in agreement with the proposal. No one member or a minority may block a decision.

C. If there is no concordance, the Leader will call for a nonbinding simple straw poll (show of hands) and further discussion. As a result of the discussion, the Leader may suggest or request modifications and check again for concordance.

D. Following the modifications, the Leader will check again to determine if there is concordance or lack of substantial agreement. If not, the Leader will ask for a show of level of support as a multiple-choice nonbinding poll.

E. After the polling, the members will be asked to voice their concerns and suggest a change in the proposal that would result in their support for the proposal, or at least move up a level in support.

F. If there isn't enough time or interest to continue discussing the issue, the group can "vote whether to vote." A _____% majority approval is necessary to require a dual (yes or no) vote. When a dual (yes or no) vote is taken, a _____% majority (concordance) is required to pass the proposal.

G. Votes may be by show of hands or written ballot. Any member may request a written ballot.

H. If more than one proposal is being considered, the group may decide to use a plurality vote and the proposal with the highest number of votes will be approved.

Rule 10: Ending the Meeting (See Roberta, Chapter Eight)

A. There will be time on the agenda at the end of the meeting for the Leader to summarize the progress made at the meeting in relation to the organization's mission or goals.

B. The Notetaker will summarize the agreements made and the follow-up action steps agreed to by the group, clarifying the tasks, the person(s) responsible, and the time limits.

C. The members will remark on their personal experience (meaning, learning, or impressions) of the meeting and make suggestions on what to continue doing or change to improve future meetings. The Leader and Egalitarian will implement feasible ideas at the next meeting.

D. When the agenda is complete, or the time established for the end of the meeting is reached, the leader will close the meeting. The meeting can continue after the established time limit elapses only if there is substantial agreement to extend the meeting for a specified time period.

E. The Notetaker will produce a brief meeting summary and action plan and send them out to the other members within _____ time period.

This is the end of the Meeting Rules Template, unless you wish to add additional sections. Please refer to to the example in the Resources (next section) for how one organization customized these rules.

Agenda for Step Eight

Sections	Method or Directions	Estimated Time
Transition	Refreshments and conversation	15–30 min.
Start the meeting		
Roles	Answer questions in item #1 of the Step Eight Worksheet	1 min.
Purpose, Checklist of Results	Review purpose and meeting checklist	5–10 min.
Agenda	Review the full agenda; adjust times as needed	
Courtesy Guidelines	Review and agree or modify	
Introduction	Read aloud; complete #2	10–15 min.
Quorum	Complete #3	10–15 min.
Decision making	Complete #4	10–15 min.
Preparation and notes	Complete #5	5–10 min.
Customize the rules	Complete #6	5–10 min.
Reflect on your progress	Complete #7	5–10 min.
Conclude	Complete #8	5–10 min.

Step Eight Worksheet

Please complete these questions and directions.

1. **Rotate Roles**

2. **Introduction**

   • Read aloud the introductions and material before "Roberta's Rules for Meetings" above.

   • Is your group the right size and the appropriate governing group to use these rules?

   • What group will these rules be used for? (Check all that apply.)

   A board _____; a council _____; committees _____; work groups or teams _____

3. **Decide on a Quorum**

   • These decisions will need to be made by your governing body before customizing these rules:

     • What will you use as a quorum for these meetings? _____

     • A quorum means that enough people are present to make a fair decision that the rest will be asked to support. Unless otherwise stated in the Bylaws, a quorum is 50% of the board or the membership required to vote. An organization may specify a smaller or larger percentage, but not usually fewer than one-fifth of the group.

     • Remember, a quorum needs to be present to make a decision (close), not to generate ideas (open) or weigh or sort ideas (narrow).

     • For a proposal to be voted on, a quorum must be present, or there must be an opportunity for those not present to vote in advance or as a continuation of the meeting. Votes may also be taken electronically if provided for in the Bylaws.

4. **Agree on Decision-Making Method**

   • Will you be using consensus or a level of "substantial agreement" (called concordance) as your primary decision-making method? _____

   • If you use concordance, what will be the percentage needed of those voting, with a quorum, to make a decision? _____ (Example: a board of twelve members with a quorum of six, or 50%, and a concordance level of 75% will need to have four people agree to pass a proposal.) Be aware that a low quorum means a very small number of people can decide for a large governing body.

   • If you choose to use consensus, what will be your written process each time? (Put this into a Governance Notebook with your Articles of Incorporation and Bylaws.) _____

   • If you choose to use consensus and can't reach it within a stated period of time, what will be your backup plan? (Example: majority rule or 50% plus one, or the standard super

majority of two-thirds, or a higher substantial majority of 75%, or four-fifths or 80%).
_____

- How long is **too long** for this group to strive to reach consensus? _____

5. Decide on Meeting Preparation and Notes

- How soon shall the Notetaker send out the meeting notes to all involved? _____

- How will meeting information be distributed in advance? By e-mail _____
On the web via _____ or regular mail_____

- How far in advance will the board members receive the agenda and prereading?
_____

6. Customize Your Rules

- Using the decisions you've made above, read and fill in the missing information in the template for Roberta's Rules for Meetings. (This template is available in Microsoft Word; please see the Resources section.)

- Make any modifications and circulate a draft for comments and feedback to all involved or affected by these changes. When done, adopt these rules using the current decision-making method stated in your Bylaws.

7. Reflect on Your Experience

- How did we do in completing this Guide? _____

- What did we do well throughout this process? _____
_____

- What did we learn and improve as we went along? _____
_____

- What did we learn that we want to incorporate into our regular meetings? (Reach agreement.)
_____
_____

8. Conclude

- Return to the Checklist of Results at the beginning of this section and check all items.

- Wrap up.

- What needs to be done to prepare for our shift to Roberta's Rules of Order and the related changes in our meetings? _____

- Are there any actions to complete to follow up this meeting?

What to Do	By Whom	By When

CONGRATULATIONS! YOU'VE COMPLETED ALL EIGHT STEPS OF THIS GUIDE AND HAVE NOW ADOPTED YOUR CUSTOMIZED RULES FOR MEETINGS, BASED ON *ROBERTA'S RULES OF ORDER.*

THIS IS A GOOD TIME TO PLAN A CELEBRATION! USE THE ACTION PLAN BELOW.

What to Do	By Whom	By When

Notes:

Resources Section

Example of a Customized Version of Roberta's Rules for an Organization

As the Board of Directors of ABC, we want to come to agreement about how we will operate and make decisions. Instead of following the standard Robert's Rules of Order, we are developing our own Guidelines for Meetings, based on *Roberta's Rules of Order,* which are less formal, more flexible, easier to remember, and closer in alignment with our organization's culture and values.

With these proposed Guidelines we are:

- [ ] Focusing on shared values and cooperation
- [ ] Creating a structure with little hierarchy
- [ ] Sharing responsibility with clear roles
- [ ] Striving for consensus or substantial agreement

This draft was prepared by staff as a starting point for the board conversation. We inserted two specific parameters as placeholders: requiring 51% of members to be present for a quorum and defining "concordance" or "substantial agreement" as at least 75% of members present.

Please review these draft guidelines and come prepared to recommend the changes you would want to make in order to vote in favor of adopting them.

We have also included suggested formats for communications and record keeping tools, as well as drafts of a Board Member Service Agreement and board Communication Agreement. These tools have been adapted from *Roberta's Rules of Order* by Alice Collier Cochran (Jossey-Bass 2004).

Example: Guidelines for Meetings for an Organization

Guideline 1: Use of Guidelines

(a) These Guidelines for Meetings are to be used as the regular Board meeting method for Organization ABC.

(b) These Guidelines may be further modified by concordance, or "substantial agreement" of the Board of Directors. (We define this as 75% of members present.)

Guideline 2: Meeting Roles

(a) The President of the organization, or a member (s)he appoints will preside at the meeting and be called the Facilitator. (S)he will appoint a Timekeeper and a Notetaker.

(b) (S)he is responsible for conducting a focused meeting that supports all voices being heard according to the Communication Agreements.

(c) All participants will help create and be asked to uphold the meeting Communication Agreements. Participants will strive to reach a consensus agreement, but if it cannot be reached within a reasonable time, the final decision will be made by concordance.

(d) The Notetaker will take brief notes during the meeting. As "tangent topics" come up, (s)he will make a list for future discussion. (S)he will write a summary of the meeting and distribute it to members within one week by e-mail.

(e) The Timekeeper will keep the Facilitator and the group aware of time. If the group has agreed upon a specified time limit for any individual to speak, the Timekeeper will give them a one-minute warning. At the end of the time, they will be asked to stop.

Guideline 3: Meeting Agenda

(a) The President or Facilitator, with suggestions from the members of the group, will draft an Agenda. This will include the meeting purpose and the meeting objectives or intended results.

(b) There will be a stated expected start and end time, list of topics, estimated time limits in minutes for each topic, the name of the person leading each topic, and the desired outcomes of the discussion.

(c) Whenever possible, the Agenda and other pertinent material will be distributed in advance by e-mail.

Guideline 4: Quorum

(a) A quorum is not required to hold a meeting. However, no decisions can be made that obligate the whole group without a quorum present in person or connected electronically. For this organization, a quorum is defined as 51% of members.

(b) If a quorum is present at the beginning of the meeting (officially determined by the President) and the agenda includes items to be decided, the decision making can continue even if members leave and a quorum is no longer present. Effort will always be made to discuss important topics while a quorum is present. Members who are absent will be informed afterward of the discussion and decisions made.

Guideline 5: Electronic Meetings and Attendance

(a) Members who cannot conveniently attend a meeting due to distance or logistical problems may attend any meeting electronically as long as everyone can be heard clearly. A designated person will make the arrangements and the costs will be covered by the organization.

Guideline 6: Starting the Meeting

(a) The tone of the meeting will be informal and friendly. Members will be given a chance to relax, with social time preceding the meeting to allow a 15-to-30-minute transition period.

(b) There may be an invocation, spiritual practice, moment of meditation, or reflection to set the tone.

(c) There will be an opportunity in the beginning for everyone to check-in briefly and update the group on any personal news or to make announcements of interest to the group.

(d) The group will review the meeting purpose, objectives, and roles at the beginning of the meeting. Members will be given a chance to read and modify the agenda at that time. The group will reach concordance before proceeding.

Guideline 7: Discussion of Issues and Proposals

(a) Any Board member (or group of members) may present a verbal or written proposal to the Board for consideration.

(b) Members are encouraged to inform the President of any issues and proposals for the agenda prior to the meeting. However, any item may be discussed that is on or added to the agenda prior to, at the beginning of, or during the meeting.

(c) The member(s) who presents a proposal for consideration should present it in the form of a simple (verbal) or structured (written) proposal. Proposals should address the problem and its causes before the solution. When possible, written structured proposals will be available for members to read in advance of the meeting. (See the QuickStart Guide to Roberta's Rules for a template.)

(d) All members will be given an opportunity to speak or ask questions. When discussing a proposal, the President or Facilitator will structure the discussion to proceed from opening (idea generation) to narrowing (evaluating ideas) to closing (making decisions).

(e) The Facilitator will ensure that all points of view are heard and considered.

(f) Any member can suggest changes to a proposal. The proposal can be modified by group concordance. If the changes are not agreed upon, another member may present a different proposal.

Guideline 8: Decision Making

(a) All members will be given an opportunity to speak at least once on each proposal.

(b) After a proposal has been presented and thoroughly discussed, the Facilitator will ask if the group is in agreement with the proposal.

(c) If there is no concordance, the leader may call for a non-binding simple straw poll (show of hands) and further discussion. As a result of the discussion, the Facilitator may suggest or request modifications and check again for concordance.

(d) Following the modifications, the Facilitator will check again to determine if there is concordance or lack of substantial agreement. The Facilitator may use one or more of several strategies to move the group toward concordance (or consensus), including multiple choice polls, inviting concerns to be voiced, and asking for additional suggested modifications to the proposal.

(e) If there isn't enough time or interest to continue discussing the issue, the group can "vote whether to vote." A 51% majority approval is necessary to require a dual (yes/no) vote. When a dual (yes/no) vote is taken, a 75% majority (concordance or substantial agreement) is required to pass the proposal.

(f) Votes may be by show of hands or written ballot. Any member may request a written ballot.

(g) If more than one proposal is being considered, the group may decide to use a plurality vote and the proposal with the highest number of votes would be approved.

Guideline 9: Executive Session

(a) Every agenda will include time (at least 60 minutes) for an executive session toward the end of the meeting.

(b) The President will determine whether to use the time and who will be invited to participate in the executive session (other than Board members). In general, the executive session will include board members and the Executive Director. Any Board member may request time without the Executive Director.

Guideline 10: Ending the Meeting

(a) There will be time on the agenda at the end of the meeting for the Facilitator to summarize the progress made at the meeting in relation to the outcomes stated on the agenda.

(b) The Notetaker will summarize the agreements made and the follow-up action steps agreed to by the group, clarifying the tasks, the person(s) responsible, and their time limits.

(c) The members will remark on their personal experience (meaning, learning, or impressions) of the meeting and make suggestions on what to continue doing or change to improve future meetings. The President and Facilitator will implement feasible ideas at the next meeting.

(d) When the agenda is complete, or the time established for the end of the meeting is reached, the Facilitator will close the meeting. The meeting can continue after the established time limit only if there is substantial agreement to extend the meeting for a specified time period.

(e) The Notetaker will fill out a meeting summary and action plan and send it out to the other members within a one-week time period.

Meeting Communication Agreements

☐ When the meeting is going off track, ask the leader to make a process check, to redirect the discussion to the topic at hand.

☐ Limit comments and conversation with those sitting near you in order not to distract others.

☐ Stay focused on the agenda and avoid jumping ahead to other issues.

☐ Turn off cell phone ringers. If you must make or return a call, leave the room.

☐ If you know you'll have to leave early, tell the group at the beginning of the meeting.

☐ Share the floor, allowing others a chance to speak on a topic before speaking a second time.

Resources from Organizations: Sources

The following organizations gave permission to use their concepts or materials in this Guide.

Interaction Associates (IA) Interaction Associates is a global provider of collaborative change consulting and workplace learning solutions. It is the first firm of its kind to fund and support a nonprofit institute, the Interaction Institute for Social Change.

Website: InteractionAssociates.com

Interaction Institute for Social Change (IISC) The Interaction Institute for Social Change provides training, consulting, and facilitation services to community leaders, nongovernmental organizations, and other nonprofit groups that are committed to social justice and civic responsibility.

Website: InteractionInstitute.org.

Community at Work Community at Work specializes in training people in the skills and concepts of group decision making and collaborative process design to reach sustainable agreements.

Website: CommunityAtWork.org

Additional Resources

For more information about organizations that provide management support or training and development, locate Resource H on pages 287–291 called "Roberta's Web Resources" in *Roberta's Rules of Order.*

Resources from Alice Cochran

How to Customize the Templates

If you have purchased a QuickStart Guide, you may obtain a copy of any template in in Microsoft Word, so that you can customize it for your group. Please contact me at Alice@RobertasRules.com

How to Order the QuickStart Guide and Roberta's Rules

This *QuickStart Guide* is available to order in hard copy (workbook format) and online from LuLu.com and Amazon.com. Please contact me if you have any difficulty finding this Guide.

The companion book *Roberta's Rules of Order* is available at local bookstores (call to order) or online at Amazon.com, Jossey-Bass.com and Wiley.com.

Become a Friend of Roberta

Please let me know how this QuickStart Guide worked well—or didn't work well—for you and your group. I would like to incorporate your feedback into the next edition. I'd also love to have any "testimonials" for the Roberta website.

To correspond with me, please send an e-mail to Alice@RobertasRules.com. I'm looking forward to hearing from you.

Notes:

Notes:

CPSIA information can be obtained
at www.ICGtesting.com
Printed in the USA
LVOW09s1328250218

567802LV00004B/169/P